The
Zero Excuses
Challenge

21 Days to Better Results in
Your Life, Career & Business

The
Zero Excuses
Challenge

21 Days to Better Results in Your Life, Career & Business

Tracie L. James

LaMorne Enterprises, LLC
2018

Just for buying this book, I want to give you a FREE gift. For more resources on how to get to zero excuses and have better results, visit **www.TracieLJames.com/zerogift**.

Dedication

This book is dedicated to my family and close friends who have stood by me throughout this journey. I am so grateful for each of you and how you've impacted my life and enabled me to fly freely into my purpose. Know that you're the wind beneath my wings and my blessings from God. I wish you all the best as you pursue your purpose.

Table of Contents

INTRODUCTION

I'm a zero and I'm proud of it!!

I know what you're thinking. What the What?! Did she really just say that? She can't seriously be proud of being a zero?

I know it seems counterintuitive to be proud of something we've been taught to see as a negative, but I'm honestly proud to be a zero. Now, let me challenge your thinking for a moment. Be open minded and let me show you why I'm so proud of being a ZERO.

I see ZERO as a great place to be. At ZERO, you're no longer negative. At ZERO, you're empty of all things negative - confusion, frustration, stress, excuses. At ZERO, you're at a point where you can launch yourself into the possibilities - new you, new career, new business, new life.

Can you see it yet?! Is it becoming clearer to you?! Not yet... let me explain further.

When I hit ZERO Excuses and I eliminated the confusion, frustration, stress and excuses in my life, career and business. Then this amazing thing happened. The whole world opened up for me and all the possibilities were in front of me. My perspective on my life and my future was changed forever. I was no longer stuck in my past failures and mistakes. I was no longer defining myself by someone else's definition of success. I no longer felt unworthy and not enough. I was finally able to see myself for who I truly am... a talented, intelligent woman who is capable of accomplishing her purpose. I am worthy. I am enough. I am exactly the woman I was created to be. I am getting better every day. What an amazing place to be!!! A place where it

didn't matter where I came from or what I'd experienced... a place where all things were possible.

HOW TO USE THIS BOOK

The Zero Excuses Challenge was not written to be a book you read and quickly forget about it. I have compiled information from my personal journey in life and business and combined it with the experiences of my clients. This book has been in development for over 20 years and you are now getting the opportunity to take full advantage of it all.

I want you to get the most out of this book. I commit to providing you with the best I have to offer that is grounded not in what I read, but what I've experienced. You must commit to investing the time and effort to take action daily to read and reflect for the next 21 days. In addition, you must commit to consistently implement the tips and strategies shared throughout this book.

This book is structured for you to read, answer questions and implement each day for 21 days. But you can attack this book in the way that suits you best. You can go at your own pace. You can read more than one day at a time. You can go in order from Day 1 to 21. You can start where you need it the most and come back to the rest later.

I recommend you set aside 30 minutes to complete each day. Be sure to have a place to take notes. There is space provided within this book or you can use a notepad & pen, tablet, computer, etc. Write down key quotes, revelations and insights that you gain as you read each chapter. Use post it notes to keep key reminders within your eyesight throughout the day.

Throughout the book, I will reference additional free resources available on my website. Utilize these resources to assist with your journey during this challenge.

What you get out of this book is a direct correlation to what you put into it. The more you put into it the faster you will get the results you want and need.

So are you ready to dive into the deep end of the pool?!

Are you ready for your ZERO Excuses moment?!

Tracie L. James

DAY ONE

What Are Excuses and Why Should I Care?

The Misson to Zero requires that you see excuses for what they really are. Excuses are familiar and we've grown comfortable with them, but they are truly dangerous to your ability to be successful. You must accept the fact that excuses are not benign issues that have to just be accepted as a part of life. Excuses are like a cancer slowly killing your self-esteem from the inside out. To get to Zero Excuses, you must stop excuses in their tracks.

You might be saying to yourself that you don't make excuses. You have reasons for why you're not pursuing your goals. So what is the difference between an excuse and a reason? Let's take a look at that by first defining the two words. Merriam-Webster's dictionary defines them:

Excuse – 1: the act of excusing; 2a: something offered as justification or as grounds for being excused; 2b excuses plural : an expression of regret for failure to do something; 2c : a note of explanation of an absence; 3: justification, reason

Reason – 1a : a statement offered in explanation or justification gave reasons that were quite satisfactory; b : a rational ground or motive a good reason to act soon; c : a sufficient ground of explanation or of logical defense; especially : something (such as a principle or law) that supports a conclusion or explains a fact the reasons behind her client's action; d : the thing that makes some fact intelligible : cause the reason for earthquakes

Based on these definitions, an excuse equals a reason that is justified. So an excuse can only be a reason if it's justifiable. You do not want to get caught in a cycle of trying to justify all of your excuses. If you're not living the life you say you want and you're feeling unfilled, frustrated and unhappy, then you must face up to the excuses you're making. My goal is to shift your mindset from trying to justify the excuses to working to eliminate them - being proactive instead of reactive; finding solutions not excuses.

Excuses affect how you think about the goals you're setting. Excuses affect how you approach the plan you've made to accomplish your goals. If you do not change your mindset, you will get caught in the excuses and never perform to your highest potential. It doesn't matter what the root cause of the excuse is, you still have to move on past it. Courage is not being without fear. It's about moving despite the fear.

It's easier to accept the excuses than to do the work to face your fears and doubts. The journey to success is not easy, but you can make it there. You just have to do it regardless. Put in the work even when you're afraid or doubt whether you and your team can accomplish the goals you've set. Don't give up. You've come this far. You shouldn't give up now. Take the leap. Be courageous and go after it with everything you have.

Personal responsibility is the antidote for excuses. You must commit to shifting the culture from one of blaming to one of personal responsibility and accountability. As an Excuse Proof Leader, you will not accept anything less. Your team will work harder and be more engaged when they take full responsibility not only for their role on the team, but also for the results achieved. Each person will have a great sense of accomplishment with each goal reached. This will be the motivation for them to keep striving. Keep leading them to each new level.

DAY 1 REFLECTION

Examine Your Own Excuses

Before I can get you to Zero, we must address the elephant in the room... the negative self-talk and the excuses that you've been using for years to downplay who you are and what amazing talents you bring to the table.

1. Make a list of the excuses you make at work, about your health, and achieving your life goals. What thoughts popped into your mind whenever you consider doing something different?
2. Consider why you make each of them.
3. Write down the worst case scenario for your life. What's the worst that could happen if you were to succeed and live the life you want?
4. Assess what you've written down for #2 and #3. Do you see a recurrent theme? If so, what is it?
5. What's REALLY blocking you from success?
6. How can you overcome what's blocking you?

Make a commitment to eliminate the root cause of the excuses you make. If there is more than one root cause, then focus on one at a time. Remember daily action builds to create the quantum leap you need to change and be more successful.

DAY TWO

Your Past Does Not Define You

In life, you have experiences that make an impact on you either positively or negatively. There's no way to avoid the negative experiences, but what you can do is not allow them to define who you are. You are not the sum of your experiences. You are the sum of your decisions. You must decide how you will respond to your past and how you will allow it to impact your future. You're on a mission to zero excuses. Don't use your past as an excuse to ruin your future.

You're probably thinking that's easy for you to say you have no idea what I've been through. Well, I can say the same to you. I could've decided to allow my past to determine who I am. Well, I've decided to stand on my past to build my future. I am the child of a teen mom who became a teen mom and didn't meet my father until I was 29. I am a divorced mother of two sons who has battled low self-esteem and depression. I have spent a huge portion of my dating life in and out of emotionally and verbally abusive relationships because I didn't embrace my worth and value. So know that what I'm sharing here is coming from a real place of understanding how your past can cloud your view of the future.

This is not meant say your problems don't exist or to move them to the side, make light of them, or diminish them in comparison to mine or anyone else's. I share this is to let you know that you aren't alone. This is to let you know that you can, and will, rise. This is intended to encourage you so you have the motivation you need to get to zero.

Make the decision to learn from your past and use those lessons to build the future you want. No matter where you come from or what you've been through you can be successful. To get to zero, you must deal with your past head on and leave it there. The more you try to ignore it without really addressing the issues the less you will accomplish in your life, career or business.

DAY 2 REFLECTION

Dealing with Your Past

1. What have you faced in your past that was difficult to overcome?
2. What experiences in your past still color your view of the future?
3. What lessons did you learn from these experiences?

Don't allow your past to hold you hostage. Take control of how you see your past. Your past does not have to dictate your future unless you allow it. We will discuss this further later in the challenge.

Tracie L. James

DAY THREE

Forgiveness

Yesterday, you dealt with your past by facing the experiences from your past that have been coloring your present and ultimately your future. You can't fully walk away from your past if you don't deal with forgiveness. I'm not just talking about forgiving others for hurting you, but also forgiving yourself for past mistakes. To get to zero, you must forgive.

Let's first address how to forgive yourself. This is often the most difficult part of the process because we tend to be harder on ourselves than anyone else ever could. When we make mistakes, we often have difficulty letting it go. It will cloud our future decisions. There are times where this can be beneficial if you learned a lesson, but if it causes you to be stuck and not grow then it's not beneficial at all. Your goal should be to grow and learn from every experience good or bad. This should occur when you make a mistake or do something you know is wrong. You must acknowledge it and learn how to not repeat the same mistake again. Life is a journey and you should learn something new every day. Perfection doesn't exist. Just be the best you that you can be each day... no more, no less.

On the other hand, you've heard it said many times that not forgiving others is like taking poison and expecting the other person to die. They have moved on with their lives and many times are not even aware that you're still upset and hurt by what happened. Let's be honest they really don't care if you're upset or not. They've moved on and you must do the same. To do so, you must forgive them. If you forgive them, you will become bitter and remain bound to the past experience. When you truly forgive, you're not saying what they did wasn't wrong or that it didn't hurt you. You're releasing the anger and hurt so it can be replaced by a feeling of joy and freedom. It's more for you than it will ever be for them, especially if you never tell them that you've forgiven them.

DAY 3 REFLECTION

Forgive Yourself

1. What have you done in the past that you need to forgive yourself for?
2. Write them down on a blank piece of paper.
3. Once you're done, writing them down. Fold the paper so you can't see what's written on the inside.
4. Say this out loud "I Forgive Myself for everything listed on this paper and everything I didn't recall. I'm starting over with a clean slate."
5. Tear up the paper into the smallest pieces possible. Keep tearing until you feel a complete release from the weight you've been carrying.

Forgive Others

1. Who has done you wrong in the past?
2. Write down each of their names on a blank piece of paper.
3. Once you've completed your list, I want you to repeat this out loud for each person on the list. "I Forgive (insert name) for hurting me. I release all the pain and bitterness associated with this experience. If I never receive an apology, I'm ok because I'm no longer holding on to (insert name)."
4. Tear up the paper into the smallest pieces possible. Keep tearing until you feel a complete release from the weight you've been carrying.

Tracie L. James

DAY FOUR

Your Character Counts

When you accepted the mission to zero, you decided to push yourself to do more than is expected of the average person. This journey will reveal who you really are. No matter what success you achieve based on your natural gifts and talents, your character will either help or hinder your progression. Your character truly counts. Your character is a combination of who you are naturally combined with your experiences during your formative years, your morals and values and your environment. There are key character traits that are essential for you to be able to maintain any level of success you achieve in your life, career or business.

It's important for you to properly develop your character by working on it daily. Your character is who you are. While your reputation is who people think you are. When you operate in your character, your reputation will line up without any problem.

I've outlined 8 character traits that will help you develop into the kind of person you would be proud to be:

1. Integrity – it's what you do when you don't think anyone's watching
2. Honesty – speak truth to yourself and others
3. Loyalty – every relationship in your life whether business or personal requires it
4. Respect – treat others decently

5. Responsible – take responsibility for your actions, feelings and emotions
6. Humility – be confident without feeling the need to bring others down to make yourself look better
7. Compassion – be an empathetic person by showing concern for others
8. Authenticity – be your authentic self and don't pretend to be anyone else to make someone else more comfortable with your presence.

Remember character development requires daily practice. You must put in the work if you truly want the results.

DAY 4 REFLECTION

Operate Within Your Character

1. Your values have an impact on your character. Take a moment and identify your 5 Core Values.
2. Then rank your values in order of importance.
3. Identify where your life is a reflection of your core values.
4. Identify where your life is NOT a reflection of your core values.
5. What are you willing to do to get your life in line with your core values?
6. What are you willing to do to keep your life in line with your core values?

If you're stuck and unsure of what your core values, visit www.TracieLJames.com/zerogift for a list of examples.

Tracie L. James

DAY FIVE

Your Mindset

Have you ever wondered why some people seem to shine anywhere they go and others cannot manage even a glimmer despite obvious talent? Research has shown that it comes down to the way that they think about their ability. So their dedication to working hard coupled with their belief in their ability enables them to succeed regardless of the situation.

To get to zero excuses, you must shift your mindset. You will not eliminate any excuses, if your mindset is negative and fixed. You must be intentional to develop a positive mindset for growth.

According to Dr. Carol Dweck, there are two ways to view your intelligence or ability:

People with a Fixed Mindset believe that ability it is fixed or ingrained. They believe we are born with a certain level of ability and no matter what we do we cannot change that.

People with a Growth Mindset believe that we can develop our ability through hard work and effort.

These two different beliefs lead to different behavior, and also to different results. If you believe you can do better and work at it, you will get better results than the person who believes that they can't do any better.

So what's your mindset? Fixed or Growth? Do you know?

There are many ways you can shift from a fixed mindset to one of growth.

#1 Develop a new belief – Begin to believe that your skills and talents can be honed by consistent effort and enjoyment.

#2 View failure as a learning opportunity – Failure is an experience not a definition of who you are. Failure is an opportunity to learn what not to do and get closer to knowing what to do.

#3 Know your strengths – Be focused on building your strengths. Abandon the idea of improving your weaknesses. When you function fully in your strengths, they will lessen the effect of your weaknesses.

#4 Learn something new every day – Make a commitment to learn at least one new thing every day. The more you learn the more you build your confidence about your skills and abilities.

#5 Challenges are positive experiences – When faced with a challenge, see it as an opportunity to ignite your creativity to find a solution to overcome the challenge.

Overall, know that you can change your mindset and positively impact your ability to accomplish your goals consistently. Each of us has a desire to achieve; we just have to take action consistently to make it happen.

DAY 5 REFLECTION

Developing Your Mindset

Key Question: Are you happy? If so, what makes you happy? If not, what is missing that would make you happy?

No one's life is perfect, but you always have something or someone to be grateful about. Consider each area and identify at least one thing you're grateful for.

Family	Relationship	Physical
Financial	Professional	Spiritual

1. Did anything surprise you about going through this process?
2. Was it easy to think of something?
3. Was it difficult for some areas?
4. Were there any recurrent themes?

Commit to express gratitude daily. Gratitude will shift your perspective and increase the joy in your life.

- What do you currently do to express gratitude? How often? How does it make you feel when you do?
- If you do not currently do anything to express gratitude daily, what will you do to bring more gratitude into your life?

I have outlined 6 strategies that I use to bring more gratitude into my life. Visit www.TracieLJames.com/zerogift to learn more about my strategies.

Tracie L. James

DAY SIX

Resilience

In life there will be times where we will be rejected – jobs, relationships, etc. We all have to deal with not getting what we want in life at times. How you deal with it is the true test of being successful. People who are resilient get through these times better. It's so important to develop resilience. Resilience is your ability to bounce back from disappointment and painful situations that occur in life. How well do you bounce back from being rejected?

One of the most important keys we must have is the power of resilience. You must develop a love for yourself enough to fight for yourself no matter what happens. You must make a decision to have the courage to push through whatever you're going through. To never give up on yourself, even when it doesn't look like it's going to work out. Discover the superhero inside of you. You are your own SUPERHERO.

Understand Resilience
Resilience is defined as the capacity to withstand life's stresses, challenges, and catastrophes. It is the ability to bounce back, to rise, and to cope when others fall apart under the same set of challenges. There is a quote by Maya Angelou that I love. I actually have it on my wall. "Surviving is important, but thriving is elegant." Thriving is my goal in life. I hit a point in my life where I decided to stop surviving and embrace thriving. I haven't looked back since.

You can never be happy in life if you do not know how to successfully rebound from life's storms. It's not if storms will come, but when. You must be prepared for the storms and be ready to stand against them.

These factors can help you build resilience:
- Close relationships with family and friends
- Embrace your value, your worth
- Effectively manage strong feelings and impulses
- Develop conflict resolution skills
- Control of your emotions
- Take personal responsibility for your choices and actions
- Avoid having a victim mentality
- Develop positive ways to cope with stress
- Being optimistic and looking for the good in even the worst situation

Find Your Resilience
Be intentional when dealing with rejection. Carolyn Gregoire in her article, "How to Bounce Back from Failure—Over and Over Again," she outlines seven traits that resilient people possess:

- They are realistic but are also optimistic.
- They don't take rejection personally.
- They create strong support systems.
- They notice the "small," positive things of life, like flowers or running streams of water.
- They practice gratitude daily.

- They seek out opportunities to improve and grow as people.
- They work through their emotions and feelings instead of avoiding them.

Look at yourself honestly and see how many of these traits do you possess. Which of these traits can you develop with focused effort? Remember we are in a growth mindset... we can change it.

DAY 6 REFLECTION

Building Your Resilience Muscle

Take some time to think about rejections you dealt with in your life. Assess them honestly by answering these questions.

1. What was the worst part about being rejected?
2. What were the benefits of being rejected?
3. Which rejection(s) permanently ruined your life and/or ability to be successful?

If you want to test your resilience muscle, there is an exercise available at www.TracieLJames.com/zerogift

DAY SEVEN

Why You Do What You Do

So many people want to know their life's purpose and have no idea where to even start. The drive to find it is a part of who we are and most will spend their entire life never knowing their purpose. This lesson is will help you to focus in on key factors so you can re-connect with who you are and find your purpose... or your why.

Before we get into the process of finding your why, let's take a moment to lay a foundation about why it's important for you to know your purpose. There are many reasons why it is important to us to seek out our life's purpose. I have outlined 5 key reasons for why knowing our life's purpose is important.

1. Unlock Your Full Potential
Knowing your life purpose will unlock within you your true potential, your natural talents. The process of knowing your life's purpose involves identifying and unlocking your gifts which will lead you to living life as your highest and true self.

You're probably using your gifts on a daily basis and be so good that you may not even know it when it is staring at you right in your face. Honestly, I was criticized for my gifts in the past and for many years I considered them a curse. Once I got clear on my life's purpose, I will able to release my gifts with confidence. Now, I use them to help others unlock their full potential.

2. Your Passion For Life

Many of us spend a huge portion of our lives feeling lost because you're not functioning in your purpose. You don't have a passion for life or for your work. This can cause you to feel tired and fatigued... Basically, you don't have joy or peace in your life.

For me, I had success professionally, but I was struggling personally. I spent so many years feeling unworthy and allowing people to treat me poorly. It was like I was living two different lives... "Superwoman" at work and "lost and depressed" at home.

Nothing came together in my life until I found my purpose, which gave me my passion for living. I finally felt alive and embraced my full worth and value. Ultimately, my entire life was transformed inside and out. Now, my work feels wonderful because I walking out my purpose. It's not always easy, but in the midst of it all I have joy and peace.

3. Money & Abundance

When you're working in your purpose, it will lead you to success and enable you to attract abundance. You will be serving the people you were born to serve. You will be creating value using your gifts and talents and you will have a deeper sense of meaning in life. Money cannot buy you happiness, but money will flow to you as a by-product of your success. When you do things in purpose, on purpose and with purpose, your work will be deeply fulfilling and gratifying... up to and including money.

4. Relationships

If you're unsure of your purpose you may have relationships may be stagnant or even fall apart. You could also feel frustration with your professional life. You're not living to your fullest potential and you're not growing. Your lack of passion for life will impact every aspect of your life in some way.

Being in line with your purpose will enable you to attract the right people into your life. The people who will support and encourage you as you walk out your purpose. Who you are and how you will your life will determine the people who come and go in your life.

5. Your Health & Wellness

When you're disconnected from your purpose, your life can be full of stress and negativity. One major benefit I received was seeing my health improve. I had struggled with weight loss for almost 10 years, but once I began to walk out my purpose the weight began to just fall off. Since my stress level dropped, stopped the "stress eating" that always involved unhealthy food. Overall, you will gain more control over your life and happiness when you live your life in purpose.

DAY 7 REFLECTION

Finding Your Why

Ground Rules – Write down your answers. Don't just think about it. If you're struggling to answer a question, skip it and come back to it later. Write the first thing that comes to your mind. Don't edit yourself. Be honest. No one else is going to read this but you.

To start this process, ask yourself these questions:

- Why is it that you do what you do?
- What thrills you about your current job or career?
- What does a great day look like?
- What does success look like beyond the money?
- What does real success feel like for you?
- How do you want to feel about your impact on the world when you retire?
- What do you hate about your current job or career?
- Why don't you do something else?
- What does a bad day look like?
- What is it you don't enjoy about your job and why?
- What does failure look like beyond the paycheck?
- What does real failure feel like for you?

Once you've answered these questions, step away. Give yourself time to process what you've written. Come back and read it later. If you skipped any questions, try to answer them when you come back.

Tracie L. James

DAY EIGHT

Who Are You?

One of the most important things you must know in life is who you are and who you are not. Your value comes from within not from outside of you. Your value is not lessened because someone else doesn't see it. You must first embrace who you are and clearly define who you are not to see your value in the right perspective.

I have worked with clients who were educated, talented, financially secure, and so much more, but they did not know their value. As a result, they often found themselves in bad relationships professionally and personally. Truthfully, for many years, I was that person. I was a woman who was very successful professionally or rather on paper. You know the right company, the right position with the right paycheck. The rest of my life was a mess. I allowed myself to be disrespected and mistreated by the people I worked with as well as my personal relationships.

I valued what others thought of me more than what I thought of myself for a long time. I finally got a revelation. I made a decision to stop shrinking myself to make others more comfortable with who I am. We were created with greatness on the inside of us and we must release it no matter what. There will always be someone who will criticize us. Remember that critics sit in the stands and pass judgment on everyone who's on the field. They aren't in the game. They are the spectators. You're in the game and you need to play with your strengths without any doubt or fear. No one else should determine your value.

You're probably wondering how I embrace my value when I have all these doubts and fears about who I am. How do I stop allowing others to dictate my value? How do I make this change and truly embrace who I am fully?

To make this happen, we must address the root cause of our doubts and fears. All of the limitations we place on ourselves come from our own minds and our own experiences. We can change this, but we must first admit we have these thoughts. You must decide to make a change for the better and move forward with confidence.

Your past is for reflection not residence. Stop living there. We all make mistakes. We all go through things in life that are out of our control. The one thing we control is how we respond to what happens in life. This response is not just about our actions, but also our thoughts. You must decide to see yourself as beautifully flawed. None of us are perfect but yet how so beautiful.

How you see yourself will impact every part of your life. How you see yourself will show others how they can treat you. How you see yourself will influence how far you can go in life. Your image of yourself will reflect in all that you do... or don't do.

You must take control of the narrative of your life. You're the producer, director, writer and star of your life. You have complete creative control. Make a decision about what you want written on the page. Make a decision about what you want to see played out on the screen. No matter what happened in the past, you still can accomplish your goals. Your dreams will still come true if you decide to not let anything or anyone stop you.

DAY 8 REFLECTION

Walking in Your Power

Answer these questions on two separate pieces of paper.

Page #1

You may want to refer to Day 2 for this exercise.

1. What past experiences (mistakes, failures, people, etc.) cloud your view of who you are?
2. What words have others spoken to you so often that the tape replays in your head constantly?

Review what you've written down and decide what lessons you learned from each experience. Once you've gleaned the lessons, then rip up the paper. Bring only the lessons with you.

Page #2

3. Write down all the things you've accomplished. Include all the obstacles you've overcome.
4. What will you do now that you can see who you are without the past clouding your judgment?

Celebrate all the things you've accomplished. Feel proud and stop allowing your past to dictate your future. It's so important to be grateful for how far you've come. Use that knowledge to give you momentum to move forward.

DAY NINE

Your Strengths...

So often the conversation is about strengths and weaknesses. Well, we're not going to have that conversation in this book. We're going to focus on your STRENGTHS. I believe that too much time is spent trying to improve weaknesses instead of capitalizing on our strengths.

I became an advocate of walking in your strengths after taking a StrengthsFinder assessment online. I began reading the research done by Dr. Donald Clifton, the Father of Strengths Psychology. Based on his study of human strengths, Dr. Clifton found that people have more potential for growth when they invest their energy in developing their strengths instead of correcting their deficiencies. His work challenged everything I had been taught over the years about focusing on your weaknesses and investing time and money to improve them so you can be more successful.

In addition, people who focus on improving their strengths are able to make more of an impact in the world. Studies conducted by StrengthsFinder showed that people who focused on their strengths every day are six times more likely to be engaged in their jobs and more than three times likely to report having an excellent quality of life. Let's be real, when you operate where you can shine you will feel better about your life and your work.

Since I've made the change to focus on investing in my strengths, I've accomplished more than I ever thought I could. Hey, you're reading my second book. I always wanted to write a book. I have started many times, but I never finished because I didn't devote the time to do it because I was busy trying to fix my flaws. I had always been considered a great writer so I had the skill needed. When I focused on improving my writing skills, I was finally able to accomplish my goal of sharing my ideas and my experience with the world. This is just one example of many that happened once I started to focus on my strengths.

During this segment, you are not expected to be humble or shy. I want you to speak boldly about what you do well... not just well, actually what do you do GREAT!! Stop hiding behind the excuse that you're not good at anything. We all have talents and skills that come so easy to us that we often overlook them. Often it's the things that people often come to you for your help and assistance. You know those things that you do for free over and over again. Those things that everyone else sees in you, but you downplay and consider to not be a big deal.

You may be sitting here thinking that I have no idea what I'm great at...Ask yourself this question:

What favors do people ask of you all the time – on your job, at church, at school, or your family?

- Are you the organizer or planner?
- Are you the peacemaker?
- Are you the writer?
- Are you the creative?

- Are you the logical one?
- Are you the teacher?
- Are you the leader?

It doesn't matter what it is. It doesn't matter if you think it's a big deal. If they're calling you for it, then you're making a difference in their lives by providing your strengths to help them accomplish their goal. Let' dig in deeper.

DAY 9 REFLECTION

Finding Your Strengths

1. What words do you hear yourself saying when someone compliments you? Are you receptive or do you consistently discount what they're saying?
2. What are you great at? What areas of your life have you been consistent?
3. In your mind, what's the most challenging thing about operating in your strengths?
4. What's the most challenging aspect of seeing yourself as an expert?

I encourage you to step into the power of your strengths. You're exactly the person the world needs right now to make change for the better happen.

If you're interested in taking the StrengthsFinder Assessment I mentioned earlier, you can access it by visiting www.strengthsfinder.com for more details on the different assessments and books available.

DAY TEN

Your Circle

General Colin Powell wrote, "Wise is the person who fortifies his life with the right friendships. If you run with wolves, you will learn how to howl. But, if you associate with eagles, you will learn how to soar to great heights."

The people on your front row, in your circle or whatever you call those closest to you, is so important to your future success. These are the people who pour into you and have the most influence on you daily. Who they are is a reflection of who you are and who you're becoming. Jim Rohn said it best when he said we are the average of the five people we spend the most time with. Today, we're going to take an honest look at your front row or inner circle.

Let's get started: I call my front row - my council. This is the group I turn to for advice, wisdom, correction, and encouragement in my life and business. They are the people closest to me - my confidantes, friends, and supporters.

I didn't always take care with the people closest to me. As a result, I often found myself hurt and betrayed by someone I "thought" cared about me. The more I worked on my personal development the more I learned how important it was to keep the right people close to you. The reality is that your network equals your net worth.

Since I began to take the time to assess my front row regularly, things have improved and I am now surrounded by people who are invested in my success. Pay attention to who's along for the ride. Be sure they aren't putting holes in your boat.

Frenemies are Real

I think as a woman I've always known that frenemies were real. Often we become numb to it because we're so used to it happening. The pain is still very real, but we often take a blind eye to the signs because we truly want to believe the person is really our friend. Unfortunately, we find out they really weren't. When a friend is not happy for your successes, you need to pay attention. Your real friends will applaud you and truly support your growth and development. They will provide correction and direction that enables you to continue your path to success. I have found through personal experience that there is a fine line between admiration and envy. Sometimes a person attaches themselves to you because they want to be you or to have your life. When they realize they can't, they will begin to turn on you – slowly and suddenly. Be sure you're having close association with people who are either where you are in life or where you want to be. Surround yourself with people who celebrate you, encourage you, and elevate you. Your front row needs to be committed to excellence and not operate in a space of jealousy.

DAY 10 REFLECTION

Assessing Your Circle

Take the time to assess your closest friendships. If you're unsure who your top 5 are, take a look at your phone log, text messages and/or social media.

1. Who are your top 5?
2. Are they the right people to help you accomplish your goals?
3. Are they encouraging you to grow and develop?
4. What changes, if any, do you need to make?
5. Are you prepared to make those changes?
6. If not, what's keeping you from making the changes?

If you determine that you have a "frenemy" on your front row, you must make the tough decision and remove them. Ask yourself these questions about this person:

- Is this person there for you when you need her? Are you likewise there for her?
- Does this person speak life to you, encourage you, and support your dreams even when you may be in doubt or fear?
- Can you count on this person to be there in all the seasons of your life, not just the good seasons?
- Does this person give you lip service? Or heart service?
- Can you trust this person with your secrets, your reputation, your life, and your heart?
- Is this person a TRUTH teller?

Once you've answered the questions, you will need to decide where they belong – a few rows back or out of your theatre completely. No need to make an announcement. Often you will not need to have a conversation with them; you just begin to change how you interact with them. You can just let time handle it. If you must have a conversation, be respectful and move on. I do my best not to burn bridges. You never know where your lives will lead and if you'll connect again in the future when they have grown.

DAY ELEVEN

Priorities Not Balance

"Your capacity is something you must be intentional about because it is at the core of how you live. The truth is we are all so busy doing what we must do, what we feel we have to do, that we never stop and take time to do the things we WANT to do." Sophia A. Nelson

I have truly learned that clearly identifying what's important in your life will enable you to know when to say "no" so you can get more done and have more joy and peace in your life in the process. Balance is a myth. The real focus should be on setting our priorities and doing those things that fall in line with those priorities. Then you are able to say "no" to the things that aren't priorities. Sounds easy, right?! It won't be easy at first, but trust me it gets easier. You just have to commit to it. This will help you build capacity in your life.

The 4 Rs of Capacity

The first step in the process is **Refuse** or rather say "no". "NO" is a complete sentence. Instead of saying I'll try, just say no. Don't stress yourself with doing things that you know you don't want to do or just don't have time to do. Don't feel guilty. Don't feel obligated to explain. The more you do it the easier it will be.

Learning to refuse is a process of setting boundaries. Time is a precious commodity and we must stop giving it away to people and activities that drain us. Focus on those people and things that inspire, encourage and motivate us.

Once you learn to say no and set boundaries, you will be able to honor "you" time, which is the second step of **Rest.** Take time to rest, not just physically, but also mentally and spiritually. and make it a part of your regular routine. It should be a priority. Start with at least 15 minutes each day to honor your mind, body and spirit. There is no "one size fits all' solution so do what works for your life. You should value this time so you can fill yourself up before you pour into others.

As a part of your routine, you will also take time for step three **Reflect.** This is your opportunity to refocus and redirect yourself and your energies. To truly be effective in getting results in your life, career or business, you must first know what direction to move in. Otherwise, you're just like the little toy wind up feet that just move around with no real direction.

Remember to be flexible. Don't let unexpected things get you off track. Reschedule priorities when life happens, but never cancel. Be creative and open to new things. You never know what's along your path to success so be open to try new things and connect with new people.

When you've completed the first three steps, you will have entered the phase of **Refresh.** You will be able to connect with people on a deeper level because you're not mentally, physically or spiritually drained. This will also create capacity for your gifts to flow freely.

Being able to build capacity in your life will able you to do what Mikki Taylor says "show up ready". Luck only happens when you're prepared for the opportunity when it presents itself. Get ready and stay ready. You will then be able to take advantage of every opportunity presented to you.

DAY 11 REFLECTION

Building Capacity

Answer the following questions:
- What are your priorities?
- What tasks or activities will enable you to honor those priorities?
- What tasks or activities do you need to remove from your schedule?

I'm sharing my daily routine with you below. There are days that I have to adjust the time, but I make sure to take time for myself each day. It doesn't matter if it's 15 minutes or two hours. I make it happen... zero excuses allowed.

Tracie's Morning Routine

4am - Wake up and pray. This is my time to be thankful for waking up.
4:15am - Meditation and hydrate. I read my devotion and drink my water & herbal tea. Sit still.
5:00am - Create my checklist. No more than 7 items for the day. I generally put 3-5 tasks. The rest that come to mind I hold for another day. I also just write and let the ideas flow.
6:00am - My son wakes up and my day begins.

Tracie's Evening Routine

9:30pm - Assess my day. Identify at least one thing to be grateful for and do a brain dump.
10:00pm - Bedtime.

- What routine will you set up for yourself starting today?
- What key activities will you include to rest, reflect and refresh?

DAY TWELVE

Be Coachable

As I've taken this journey to success, I have come to realize that successful people have something key in common. They surround themselves with people who are where they want to be in their life, career or business. They value wise counsel because they know how very important it is to being successful. They are open to receiving advice and direction. They want to learn and get better every single day.

When I decided I wanted more in my life, I knew it was time to move outside my comfort zone. Nothing good happens in the comfort zone. There is no growth in the comfort zone. There's only stagnation in the comfort zone. The real magic happens when we get outside your comfort zone. Learn to be comfortable being uncomfortable.

To truly move ourselves outside the comfort zone, we must get help. If we could accomplish our goals on our own, we would have done it already. We have gotten ourselves as far as we could on our own. To truly grow and operate in the place outside the comfort zone, you need to be coachable. You must find a mentor or coach who is where you want to be in your life, career or business.

Personally, I have a coach and several mentors. This has helped me accomplish so much more in a shorter period of time. Let me clarify who is in my group. I have a business coach who is there to help me with the aspects of my business. In addition, I have a couple of mentors who are there to provide life advice. These three people I know personally and connect with regularly. I also have mentors that I have never met before. These are public figures that I watch from a distance and learn from them. With all of these examples, I have a great foundation for success.

Let's begin work on building your group of mentors and coaches. You must be intentional and purposeful about whom you connect with for advice and direction. Keep these key points in mind as you make your selections.

Who Do You Listen To
Choose wisely. You must use discernment. These are the people that you go to for advice, support and encouragement. They need to be people who truly believe in you and your vision. They are there to have the tough conversations when needed. Remember that iron sharpens iron. People who cannot do what you can do will always criticize what you do. They will always question what you do and why you do it.

How Do You Listen
Be open to hear everything they bring to the table. You must be willing to hear those things you don't really want to hear. A real coach or mentor will tell you what you need to be successful even if it will hurt your feelings. Be willing to receive it with an open mind. Ask questions to clarify and gain a full understanding of what they are telling you. Don't just accept it. This should be a conversation, not a lecture.

The more questions you ask the better your coach or mentor can help you accomplish your goals. Your coach cannot read your mind. You must let them know if you're struggling and if you're at a loss for what you are doing.

Stay humble so you can be pressed to move your good to great and your great to best.

How to Maintain the Relationship
Stay engaged with your coach and mentors regularly. Keep them informed of your progress. Remember regardless of whether you're paying them for advice or not, they have committed themselves to your success.

In addition, be of service to your mentor, especially those who are giving of their time freely to you. If you see areas of where you can help them, then offer your assistance. If you're unsure of how you can help them, then ask them how you can be of service. They will appreciate your desire to give back to them. It creates a beautiful circle of support.

DAY 12 REFLECTION

Finding Advisors

Ask yourself these questions before seeking advisors.

1. How can I benefit from a coach or mentor?
2. Am I prepared to invest in a coach or should I focus on a mentor?
3. What can I offer to a potential mentor? How can I be of service?

The Dos & Don'ts of Finding a Mentor

1. Don't ask a stranger. Your first conversation should not be about being a mentor.
2. Do seek out a person that not only fits your career or business goal, but their life is also one you admire.
3. Do build a relationship by following their work and being supportive.
4. Do offer your service to your prospective mentor. Bring value to the table. We all have something to offer – share articles, support events, volunteer, etc.
5. After building a relationship with your prospective mentor, be respectful of their time by being specific about what you need from them.

More tips available at www.tracieljames.com/zerogift

DAY THIRTEEN

Be Courageous

At one time in my life, I wanted my fear to just go away. I was determined to find a way to get rid of every one of my fears. We all have those moments at times when we're faced with a challenge or an opportunity to do something different. We just want the fear to go away so we can move forward. We must learn that being courageous requires that the fear still be there. You cannot be courageous unless you move despite the fear or doubt.

Think about heroes in the movies. The hero faces the challenge even though they are afraid or have doubts. It's no different in life. You must be courageous and move forward even though you're afraid. I share with my clients how I took action on building my business even though I was afraid. I made phone calls, went live online and sent emails with my palms sweating, knees knocking and teeth chattering. I decided that I wanted it more than I was afraid of it.

What is that one thing that you're afraid to do? What's the one goal that keeps you stuck because of fear? Are you afraid of failing or of success? Really think about it.

Learn to use fear as your motivation. I read a book by Shonda Rhimes that has become the foundation of my decision model in life and business. If it doesn't scare me to do it, then it's inside my comfort zone and I must say "NO" to it. If it scares me to do it, then it's outside my comfort zone and I must say "YES" to it. That's right, I've decided to be comfortable being uncomfortable. The goal is to continue to press myself further with each step I take personally and professionally.

Using fear as a motivator and director has enabled me to do more than ever before. I want you to have the same ability in your life, career and business. It's important that you stretch yourself and continue to grow personally and professionally.

Now, you're probably wondering 'how can I move when I'm scared'. Listen I totally get it. I thought the same thing at first. Honestly there are still times I have the same thought. I have just decided to ignore it and move anyway. Some action is better than "perfect action" that never happens. My process now is plan, act, assess and adjust then repeat.

I encourage you to pursue that big goal relentlessly. Protect it from all negativity. You have everything you need to get started. Anything else you need you can acquire as you take action. The most important thing is to be courageous and just get started. It doesn't matter what anyone else thinks about what you're doing. The most important thing is for you to take action and never give up. Remember no matter what happens just do it regardless!!!

DAY 13 REFLECTION

Be Your Own Superhero

Answer the following questions:

1. What is the one thing you've been most afraid of doing?
2. What's the worst scenario that you have in your mind associated with this goal? (answer on a separate sheet)
3. What's the best scenario that you have in your mind associated with this goal? (answer on a separate sheet)
4. Compare your responses to questions #2 and #3. What's the theme in each? What do they have in common? What are the differences?
5. Tear up the sheet with the answer to #2.
6. Post up the sheet with the answer to #3. This is where you need to focus so you can take action on accomplishing this goal.

How to be More Courageous
1. Don't procrastinate.
2. Avoid negativity.
3. Face your fear and step outside your comfort zone.
4. Be disciplined.
5. Don't over think. Take Action.
6. Trust Yourself.
7. Focus on why you're taking action.
8. Learn from any mistakes or missteps.

Tracie L. James

DAY FOURTEEN

Authenticity

Making the decision to embrace who you are sounds easy, but it requires work and courage. Living in a world that values the superficial doesn't make it easy to truly embrace your true power that lies within you. Take the steps necessary to embrace who you are and you will find true power.

I can tell you from personal experience that when you fully embrace the power of being authentically you are is unlike anything else you've ever experienced. It feels great when you get here. The journey is what is tough. People will not understand why you don't want to fit in anymore. They will see what you're doing as weird and crazy. Ignore it and continue to tap into who you really are so you can find your purpose and success.

Today, our focus will be on three areas needed to embrace the power in authenticity:

1. What is Authenticity?
2. What Blocks Authenticity?
3. Be Authentic!

The power you have within you will enable you to accomplish every goal you set and find the success you've been looking for all this time. Being who you uniquely are will give you a competitive edge. There is no one else on earth exactly like you and that's wonderful. You will find kindred spirits, but no one exactly like you. Take the step and be authentically you.

What is Authenticity?

To be authentic is to be an original. It is to be true and not false. It is to be pure, rare, and verifiable. Most people never fully achieve authenticity because they are afraid of how others will view them. To be authentic, you must be comfortable being unique.

When you understand the power of authenticity, you are more resilient. You are less likely to turn to drugs, alcohol, or addictive habits as coping mechanisms. You are more likely to be purposeful and focused in your goals. You are more likely to follow through on your goals.

What Blocks Authenticity?

Living your life on other people's terms is at the foundation of what blocks authenticity. I am a recovering "people pleaser". I spent a huge portion of my life doing what others felt was best for me. I finally hit the wall and decided I needed to focus on what makes me happy. There is happiness and joy in being authentically you.

Do you recognize any of these situations?
- You are always doing for others. You don't even know the meaning of "me time" or "self-care".
- You never think about your needs and would never ask for them if you did.
- You are still living the dreams of your parents and/or mentors.

- You walk around with unresolved pain and heartache. You're in complete denial.
- You're working a job you hate.
- Your relationships are unfulfilling and you hate them. You feel stuck and have no idea how to make things better or to get out.

You are the only person that can make the changes necessary to create the life you really want. The life that would be authentically you – walking in your purpose – is just one decision away. Take the courageous step and begin to make changes today.

Be Authentic!
True power exists in being authentic! True power happens when you begin to operate in your life purpose. It's such a beautiful thing to see someone who is doing exactly what they were created to be. You must decide you want if for yourself more than you want to avoid the discomfort of change. Focus on discovering the real you and your real purpose. Eliminate that restless and stuck feeling by seeking your purpose. You won't find it in your comfort zone.

Redefine for yourself what success really looks like. Move away from what is conventionally accepted as success, love and living a full life. Paint your own masterpiece. Your life is your canvas. Decide what beauty you will create on it each day. Once you make the shift into being authentic, you will not want to operate anywhere else. You will be exactly who you were created to be and your life will never be the same again.

Tracie L. James

DAY 14 REFLECTION

It's time to have an honest conversation with yourself about yourself. Without considering what your family thinks, what your spouse thinks, what your friends think, or what the world demands, take into consideration only what YOU think.

1. Make a list of the things in your life that are most important to you that you want to continue.
2. Add to the list all of the things that are not currently part of your life that you want to add.
3. Develop a strategy to make this list a reality.

How you can make your desired life a reality:
1. Operate in your worth and value. Make decisions about that reflect your worth and value consistently. (Refer to Day 8)
2. Find your purpose in life. Knowing your why will help you build the life you desire.
3. Don't be afraid to make a major change in your life personally or professionally. No matter how old you are or how long you've been doing something. It's never too late to make a change.
4. Trust yourself to know what to do. Stop second guessing. Your instincts tend to be right. The more you trust them the more they will guide you in the right direction.
5. Face your past. Learn your lessons and move forward. (Refer to Day 2)
6. Keep your inner circle full of people who love, support and encourage you to be authentically who you are.

Tracie L. James

DAY FIFTEEN

Habits

I'm so excited that you have made it this far on this journey. You're in the home stretch and now we're taking action on all the things we've covered the last two weeks. Today, we're going to focus on changing your habits. We've looked at key elements you need to be more successful. The key now is to create the environment in your life to support each of those qualities.

Before you can break the cycle of bad habits, you must understand how habits work. Scientists have proven that habits are formed and operate entirely separate from the part of our brain that is responsible for memory. We learn and make unconscious choices without having to remember anything. Our brains are constantly looks for shortcuts and "chunks" sequences of actions into automatic routines.

The habit loop as described in the book "The Power of Habit" shows a sequence of cue, routine, and reward. The more you study this loop you will begin to recognize the cues that you respond to and send you into the routine of making excuses. You can't interrupt the cycle until you identify what your cues are. What happens right before you begin to make excuses?

Habits can only be changed if a new routine is successfully inserted into the process with the same cue and the same reward. The first key is to insert a new routine into the cue/reward sandwich by identifying what need the reward is fulfilling and providing a similar type of relief through a new routine. The less complicated the routine the easier it is to replace the bad habit with a better one.

For example, at one time my routine for dealing with a stressful day was to drink wine and eat a heavy, unhealthy meal. The drinking and eating made me feel good, relaxed and fulfilled. Now, I have replaced my wine with tea and the unhealthy meal with one that energizes me. The cue is still the stressful day and I still get the same feelings. It took some time to change my routine, but it's much easier now because I have an added result of weight loss and more energy after this new routine.

My routine changed worked for me for two main reasons I found a less complicated way to get the same results, but I also believed I could do it. I made a decision that this was better for me in the long run and it stuck with the help of my front row. They supported my decision and helped me make the change. Don't get me wrong I still enjoy a glass of wine, but it's now not in response to a stressful day. I know have a glass of wine as a part of a good meal or celebration. As a result, I drink less and with a healthier meal.

What routines do you need to change to get better results than you're currently getting? Do you believe that you can make the change? Do you have the support around you to help you make the change? Let's take some time today to think about our habits and begin the process of replacing them one by one.

WARNING – Do not try to change more than one habit at a time. It takes time to truly change your routine. You will have setbacks at times, but the most important thing is that you do not allow them to stop you from continuing to move forward to make the necessary changes for you.

DAY 15 REFLECTION

Developing the Right Habits

1. Identify one habit that you want to change.
2. What is your cue?
3. What is the result you get from the routine/habit?
4. What routine can give you the same result?
5. Start today, making the changes to your routine by sharing your plan with an accountability partner.

Once you accomplish changing the first habit, then you will have the momentum you need to make the next change. Before you know it, you will have built a new series of habits that support your new life of living at Zero Excuses.

TIP – If you're unsure of where to start with your habits, I encourage you to begin with how you start and end your day. If your day starts off on the right foot, then you can handle whatever the day throws at you. If you end your day in the right mindset, then you will rest well and have a better morning the next day. It's a cycle that keeps on giving either positively or negatively. I've shared my routines with you in Day 11. Refer back to them as a template.

DAY SIXTEEN

How You Talk to Yourself

Self-talk is "the act or practice of talking to oneself; either aloud or silently and mentally." Keeping this self-talk positive, uplifting and motivating will enable you to shift out of neutral. Your self-talk is central to your mindset because it brings your thoughts and words together to develop your action.

You must understand that your words have power. Be careful what you speak because you can plant exactly what you don't want to happen. Speak your success. Speak positive words over yourself, over your family, over your business, over your career. When you speak negative words, catch yourself and correct it. Speak positive words daily.

When we speak, we give others an indication of who we are, what we think, and how we feel about ourselves and the world around us. What you speak and the resulting actions you take, let people know what's really in your heart. You can change what you speak, by being purposeful with your words.

Using "I am" statements will enable you to shift from a constant feeling of "I can't" into a space of "I can". Speaking positive, present tense statements will shift your self-talk into the right place. There is power in words spoken over us, about us, and into us can last a lifetime. Words have the power to inspire, propel, or diminish us. Use your words to inspire and propel yourself into your success.

Joel Osteen says that what words you place behind "I am" will pursue you. Think about that for a moment. What do you want pursing you? Do you want success or failure pursuing you? Do you want happiness or sadness pursuing you? It's all up to you. What you think… what you speak… is what you will receive.

I'm not talking about "name it and claim it", but I'm talking about getting your mind, your words and your actions all on the same page. It's imperative that it all lines up in order for you to truly be successful consistently. Your actions follow your thoughts and words so it's so important for you to keep them in a positive space if you're truly committed to achieving your goals.

DAY 16 REFLECTION

The Beauty of Speaking Love to Yourself

Answer these questions:

1. What internal dialogue do you have when you become discouraged, afraid or doubtful about the issues in your life?
2. Which of your flaws causes you the most frustration? Are you overly focused on fixing this flaw to the point of distraction?
3. How could your life be changed by increasing your confidence? Describe your life if you were more confident.
4. What words do you speak the most over yourself? On good days? On bad days?
5. Develop your own Daily Affirmations to add to your daily routine. I speak my daily affirmations as I stand in the mirror getting dressed for the day.

Daily Affirmations
Look at yourself in the mirror and speak positive words over yourself, your family and your life. You need to learn to be able to speak positively about yourself and your talents & gifts.

I have shared my affirmations on www.TracieLJames.com/zerogift. Write your own or use mine.

Tracie L. James

DAY SEVENTEEN

Solutions Not Excuses

I'm a solutions minded person. I'm often frustrated when I get stuck in conversations about what's wrong but there are no solutions presented to address the issues. I believe that something more should happen than just venting. I believe we all have a responsibility to impact change not only in our lives, but our communities and the world as a whole. My friends often refer to me at the "fixer".

As I work with clients, I am focused on finding the right solutions for their problems. It's imperative that you begin to develop this mindset as well. It's the foundation of being excuse-proof and living with a zero excuses mentality. You can get past excuses if you're focused on creating solutions. It doesn't matter if the excuse is grounded in fear, doubt, worry, past experiences, or being uncomfortable, there is a solution to address it.

To be a great problem solver, you must learn the basic steps.

1. Identify the right problem. At times, people see the symptoms as the problem. Take the time to look for the root cause of what you're seeing on the surface.
2. Ideate for possible solutions. Just do a "brain dump" and write down all ideas that come to mind. Don't over think it. Just write it all down. No idea gets trashed at this phase.

3. Evaluate possible solutions identified. Here you can assess the feasibility of each idea. You will need to eliminate as many ideas as possible and leave the top ideas. Take your top ideas and share with your advisors and get their feedback. Then decide how to move forward.
4. Execute the selected solution. Fully implement the plan agreed upon.
5. Assess your results. Take time to evaluate how things are progressing and make changes as needed to ensure you get your desired results.

This process can take weeks or minutes depending upon the problem you're working to solve. Let's take a look at the process when dealing with an excuse.

Excuse – I don't know how to do it.
What's the real problem? Is it fear or truly a lack of knowledge?

Option #1
If it's fear, what are the possible solutions?

If it's fear, you do it anyway. Be courageous and take action using the knowledge you currently have.

Option #2
If it's a lack of knowledge, what are the possible solutions?

If it's a lack of knowledge, where can you acquire the knowledge? Degree? Certification? Apprenticeship? Mentoring?

Once you identify the best way to acquire the knowledge needed, then you take action until you get what you need to move forward.

The most important thing is that you take action, even if you have to make changes to the plan and start over.

DAY 17 REFLECTION

Be a Problem Solver

1. What is the number one excuse blocking you from accomplishing the goals you have?
2. Apply the problem solving process to this excuse to find the right solution.
3. Implement the solution until you get the results you want.

You must take the initiative to solve your own problem. If you're truly stuck, then do not hesitate to get help from someone who is where you want to be. Get an advisor, mentor, or coach. They can help you avoid some potholes and help you accelerate your progress.

DAY EIGHTEEN

Goal Setting & Effective Planning

I struggled for many years setting personal goals. I excelled at setting and achieving goals in my professional life. It took me years before I ever applied what I did in my professional life in setting goals and developing an effective plan for accomplishing my life goals. Once I began to use what I did so well at work in my life, I started to see so many positive changes. I began to live my life instead of just existing.

Today, I'm going to share with you what I do personally and what I help my clients do with their goals. Over the years, I have found the use of the S.M.A.R.T. method to be very effective for defining my goals and objectives with my teams. I now apply this same method to my life goals.

S – Specific: State exactly what you want to accomplish - who, what, where and why.

M – Measureable: Quantify the goal so that progress can be monitored.

A – Agreed Upon: Get consensus from your team; including accountability.

R – Relevant: Goals should be consistent with other goals. Be sure no conflicts exist.

T – Time-based: Set a deadline for completion of the goal. It must have an end date.

When you assess each of your goals with these parameters, you can be sure to not only have a goal, but also a pathway to that goal you want to accomplish. You can be more successful as a result. You will begin to pursue your goals without excuses.

Now that you have your goals written down, you can begin to reverse engineer your plan for accomplishing each one. Assess where you are now and where you want to be. Your plan must address what's in the gap between the two. If you just write down goals without a plan of action, then you only have half of what you need.

I will give you a weight loss example to help you understand what I mean.

Where I am NOW: I weigh 165 pounds. I do not work out. I do not eat healthy consistently.

Where I want to BE: I want to weigh 135 pounds by the end of the year. I want to work out consistently. I want to eat healthy consistently.

What's in the GAP: I need to lose 30 pounds. I need to get active. I need to make changes to my eating habits.

My Plan to Accomplish my GOAL: I will work out 5 days a week for at least 45 minutes. I will eat healthy meals 6 days per week. I will eliminate all beef, pork and chicken from my diet. I will eat only vegetables and seafood. My friend Sara will be my accountability partner. I will share my activity on

MyFitnessPal with her every day. I must lose an average of less than a pound a week to achieve my goal.

Soooo, do you see what I mean by filling in the gap with a clear plan of action that is measureable.

DAY 18 REFLECTION

Become a Strategist

1. What is your number one goal you want to accomplish?
2. Use the SMART goals method to define your goal.
3. What's in the gap between where you are and where you want to be?
4. Develop your plan and write it down.
5. Who will be your accountability partner?
6. Repeat this process for each of your goals.

DAY NINETEEN

The Importance of Accountability

One of the most challenging aspects of coaching is knowing what to do when the person I'm working with is not completing the work we've agreed upon. Since everyone's motivations are different, I ask my clients how they want me to respond in these situations. There is not a one size fits all answer to the accountability question.

One thing I know to be true is that before I can hold you accountable, you must first hold yourself accountable. Many who make excuses are caught in a cycle of blaming others for their inability to be successful and accomplish their goals. It's always someone else's fault that they are not where they want to be in their life, career or business. This attitude is detrimental in so many ways. You can never learn and grow if you never take personal responsibility for your own life and what happens in it. It doesn't matter what I do to hold you accountable if you do not first take responsibility for your actions or lack of actions.

Let's address how you begin to take personal accountability and top the cycle of blaming.

1. No matter what happens take responsibility for what you did or didn't do.
2. Fix what needs to be fixed.
3. Apologize accordingly.
4. Be clear about responsibilities and expectations upfront.

5. Stay focused on solutions. The goal is always to get results.

I know it's not always easy to be personally accountable, especially when we've made a mistake or a bad decision. I have learned from personal experience that people respect you so much more when you own your mistakes. They are more forgiving and more willing to help you make corrections. In the long run, you want to be seen as a person of integrity and who stands by their results good or bad.

Perfectionism is the root cause for those who are blame others. They are more concerned with being seen as perfect than being honest and taking responsibility. Let's shift the focus from creating perfection to operating in excellence. When you accept the fact that we all make mistakes, then we are more able to handle our own mistakes and those of others. We must strive for excellence and the desire to be better than we were the day before. Consistent growth is where excellence can be found.

DAY 19 REFLECTION

Be Accountable

1. Think about a time where you should have taken the blame for a mistake or bad results and you didn't.
2. If you were in that situation again, how would you handle it differently?
3. What can you learn from that situation now to ensure you don't blame others again?
4. Make a commitment to yourself to be accountable in all that you do. When you catch yourself blaming others, take a deep breath and own what happened.

Tracie L. James

DAY TWENTY

The Danger of the Comfort Zone

There is constant conversation around getting outside your comfort zone. There's talk, but little action by most. It's important that your focus be on growing, stretching and pressing yourself outside of your comfort zone. The real magic happens outside of your comfort zone. I've found that when I pursue something that scares me I'm blessed in the end, but I'm also stretched and I grow immensely. Today, we're going to get comfortable being uncomfortable.

It is a dangerous place to settle in your comfort zone. If you stay there, then you will never fulfill your full potential. You will never accomplish your vision. You will never truly live until you get outside of your comfort zone. Continue to push yourself to accomplish even more. Continue to learn from any failures and to press toward the next goal. Continue to strive toward excellence, not perfection. Be prepared to make adjustments as you move along.

To get and stay out, you must fully understand what these comfort zones look like.

There are three types of comfort zones:

Comfort Zone of *Success* - Once you find the success you seek, there is a risk that you will get comfortable and complacent. Remember success is a journey not a destination. The mark of success continues to move as you accomplish each goal. In success, you can begin to work on autopilot. Success continues to come but you never achieve more than you did the last time. You have officially entered the comfort zone. You are not pushing yourself anymore. You are just happy with the status quo. No one is pushing you anymore because you are still ahead or at par with your peers. Most won't expect more from you because you're still successful... just not as successful as you could be.

Comfort Zone of Failure - In contrast, there is the comfort zone of failure. You can get comfortable after you've had a series of failures. You just decide not to take any risks. You stay in that safe box where you can easily find your success again. It doesn't challenge you. It's just comfortable. You must be willing to take risks again. Use your fear as a motivator. Look for the opportunity in the fear.

Comfort Zone of Perfection - The comfort zone of perfection is a space where you are so busy trying to make things perfect or waiting for the perfect time that you never get anything done. Excellence should be the goal not perfection. Perfection is an ideal and not a reality. A desire for perfection will not get you to your goals. You never know what you have until you release it. While you are trying to make it perfect, others are taking the risk and then fixing any issues as they arise. The important thing is that they made a move and released their work in excellence.

DAY 20 REFLECTION

Avoid the Comfort Zone

1. What limitations have you placed on yourself personally and professionally?
2. What's behind these limitations? Self image? Past experience? Other people's opinions?
3. Should you allow any of these to define who you can be in the future?
4. Make a list of the things that scare you the most (goals, people, places, etc).
5. Pick one from the list to take action on today.
6. What will you do today to take action and push yourself outside your comfort zone?

Tracie L. James

DAY TWENTYONE

Welcome to Team Zero Excuses

I'm so excited that we've made it to the last day of the challenge. You've put in the work to make the change you need within you and have begun to take action. You should be so proud of yourself. I officially welcome you to Team Zero Excuses where we get more results because we decided that the last time was the last time. We're focused on solutions not excuses. We're committed to being the best we can be and live our lives to the fullest at all times.

Excuses are familiar and we've grown comfortable with them, but they are truly dangerous to our productivity and the ultimate success in our lives. Remember that excuses are not benign issues that have to just be accepted as a part of life. Unchecked excuses can prove malignant to everything you do. Excuses can be like a cancer slowly killing your self esteem, self image, productivity and success from the inside out.

You now have the tools you need to get past the excuses blocking you from getting all the success you see yourself having. You have a clear strategy that you can implement from now on to not only help yourself, but to help others. I encourage you to share what you've learned here. Bring someone else along with you to Team Zero Excuses.

When you join Team Zero Excuses, you are at the magic place of being empty of excuses yet full of the possibilities of your future. Embrace all the potential inside of you and launch yourself into your success. Stop being stuck and enjoy the journey to success that you can have when you let go of all the excuses. You're ready to blast off!! 5 4 3 2 1 0

DAY 21 REFLECTION

Launch Yourself

1. What commitments are you making to yourself to continue after this challenge ends?
2. How will you remain accountable on the goals you've set for yourself?
3. Write down your vision for where you will be 12 months from today. Make it a vivid picture including all the sights, sounds and feelings.

Tracie L. James

ABOUT THE AUTHOR

Tracie L. James is a Sales and Marketing professional turned Leadership Strategist, Corporate Trainer, Speaker, and Author of "Excuse Proof Leadership". For over 20 years, she has utilized her expertise to help corporations, nonprofits, and educational programs. Clients include executives, entrepreneurs and organizations of all sizes. Tracie has appeared on TV and radio. In addition, she has performed on stages throughout the United States.

With numerous awards and accolades throughout her sales, marketing, speaking and consulting careers, Tracie is not easily placed in one category, she defines her own. Tracie's number one goal is to educate, develop and encourage leaders to reach their full potential.

Follow Tracie on Facebook, Instagram and Twitter @iamtracieljames or visit her website at www.TracieLJames.com

To request Tracie for your next event, email Hello@TracieLJames.com

Tracie L. James